Kurt Weill

The Magic Night Waltz
from *Zaubernacht*

arranged by Meirion Bowen
for Violin and Piano

EA 850

EAM
EUROPEAN AMERICAN MUSIC
CORPORATION

The Magic Night Waltz
from "Zaubernacht"
for Violin & Piano

Kurt Weill
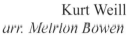

The Magic Night Waltz
from "Zaubernacht"
for Violin & Piano

Kurt Weill
arr. Meirion Bowen